SHIFT

90 DAYS OF ANOINTED PROPHETIC DECLARATIONS

BERNARD W. DESLANDES

PROPHET BERNARD
MINISTRIES

Published by: Prophet Bernard Ministries

Kingston, Jamaica

Email: prophetbernardministries@gmail.com

Website: www.prophetbernardministries.org

SHIFT: 90 Days of Anointed Prophetic Declarations

ISBN: 978-976-96025-3-3

Unless otherwise noted, Scripture quotations are taken from the Authorized King James Version of the Bible.

Editor: I-Edit (Nadine A. Thomas, M.Mgt)

Cover Design: Oliver Jordine

Contents

To all who are sensitive to their season and understands that there is an appointed time for everything under the sun.

Introduction

LIFE AND DEATH ARE IN the power of the tongue (Prov. 18:21). Whatever we say out of our mouth is powerful enough to affect our lives. We have been given the authority and creative ability from God to speak things that are not yet present in our lives into reality. This act of faith-speaking is called a declaration. This declaration is not necessarily a prophecy as coming from God, but it is the child of God participating in the prophetic process as he/she sets the Word of God into motion concerning one's life.

This awesome privilege that we have been given is, firstly, our chance to participate in the dominion rulership given to us by God. This dominion authority cannot be exercised if we do not first open our mouths and begin to say something. What we say over our lives and pronounce over our destiny is crucial. These pronouncements will go before us and begin to pave the way until we arrive at our destination.

God promises us that we will decree a thing and it will be established for us (Job 22:28). This promise is not a conditional one, but one that is absolute and governs everything that we say whether it is positive or negative.

We ought to, therefore, ensure that we constantly make positive declarations over our lives so that our future can begin to take shape based on the words that we are declaring.

This awesome privilege that we have further gives us the opportunity to partake in the shaping of our destiny to some extent. We have the opportunity to agree and partner with God in deciding what happens to us in the future. Our words are, therefore, important and we cannot allow just about anything to proceed from our mouths.

The Word of God is filled with decrees that we can make concerning our lives. These decrees are eternal as they are coming out of and linked to the Word of God. As we make those decrees we give angels assignments concerning our lives. Angels are activated whenever God's Word is decreed, and are always ready to move on our behalf (Ps. 103:20).

The earth and the universe were created by the spoken word. God called everything into being by the power of the spoken word. Nothing came into existence without a word being spoken. Before ever there was manifestation of anything there was the spoken word. This word is still upholding the universe.

The problem we are having today is that we are speaking too much of the wrong things. Anything we speak is bound to happen as words cannot return to its source but must accomplish what it is sent out to do. We are created in the image of God to act like God - well at least that's what we should be doing. Anything that God says come to pass. So why it is that we should be any different if He has created us to be like Him?

Before anything comes out of our mouths, it is first said in our hearts. Our heart is the manufacturing chamber of the words that we speak. If this is indeed the case, then what we need to do is to get our hearts aligned in such a way that whatsoever comes out of it will be words that foster and create pathways of blessings and prosperity for us.

The moment we begin to speak negatively then that will be the result. The moment we begin to speak positively then that will be the result. The spiritual atmosphere and environment around us can only respond to what we have decreed in it or what we have allowed to be decreed by others. Whatever we decree, so shall it happen.

A decree has a greater dimension than just a spoken word in the sense that a decree comes out of your spirit with a prophetic mandate. Decrees are prophetic pronouncements and whatever is prophesied will begin to act on our behalf. Why not make some decrees concerning your future? You have not gotten there yet but certainly your words will reach there before you. Words go out and they continue until they accomplish what it has been sent to do. Words are life-like and carry with them the power to cause something to happen.

What is that something that you want to happen? Why not decree it and connect your declarations to the Word of God to open the heavens in a brand new way over your life. Let your words go before you so that things can be shifted for you as the glory-realm begins to act on your behalf.

Within this book, there are *90 Days of Anointed Prophetic Declarations* from the Scriptures. Take the challenge and make each declaration over your life *twenty one times* each day or as often as you can. It is not the repetition of the declarations that causes the *Shift* but your trust and faith in God! I believe that as you do this, things will begin to change in your life as the Word of God becomes the standard for your future. God bless you as you *Shift* the atmosphere of your life and affect your future for good. I say in the Name of Jesus, *Shift*!

Ninety Days of Declarations

THE CONDITION OF YOUR heart is very important when you are speaking, as emotions give strength and expression to words. Take the time to repent and allow the Spirit of God to cleanse your heart. When you are done, go before God in worship so that the atmosphere is saturated with His praise.

Each day is tied to a theme. The declaration is connected to the Bible passage that is given above it. First, establish the theme by saying, for example, *"This is Day One, the Day of Greatness"*. Secondly, read and meditate upon the Bible passage below it. Allow the Holy Spirit to burn that specific Word into your heart. Finally, when you are satisfied, make the declaration written below twenty one times throughout the day or as often as you can and expect the Lord to move on your behalf.

Day 1
Greatness

And I will make of thee a great nation, and I will bless thee, and make thy name great; and thou shalt be a blessing:
Genesis 12:2

I shall be great in this nation. Abundance of good things and benefits shall come unto me. Great shall be my name in the land and people shall be blessed because of me, in the Mighty Name of Jesus, Amen.

Day 2
Plenty

Therefore God give thee of the dew of heaven, and the fatness of the earth, and plenty of corn and wine: Let people serve thee, and nations bow down to thee: be lord over thy brethren, and let thy mother's sons bow down to thee: cursed be every one that curseth thee, and blessed be he that blesseth thee.
Genesis 27:28-29

The heavens and the earth shall be in harmony over my life. I shall have plenty of good things. Power shall be granted unto me over my enemies and great shall be the interest of God towards me, in the Mighty Name of Jesus, Amen.

Day 3
Dew of Heaven

Therefore God give thee of the dew of heaven, and
the fatness of the earth,
and plenty of corn and wine:
Genesis 27:28

The dew of Heaven shall be over the work of my hands. It shall be fruitful and it shall be multiplied to fill this city and land, and my profit shall be great, in the Mighty Name of Jesus, Amen.

Day 4
Multiplication

That in blessing I will bless thee, and in multiplying I will multiply thy seed as the stars of the heaven, and as the sand which is upon the sea shore; and thy seed shall possess the gate of his enemies.

Genesis 22:17

My children and I shall not be cut off. Our lineage shall be great, in the Mighty Name of Jesus, Amen.

Day 5
Inheritance

And give thee the blessing of Abraham, to thee, and to thy seed with thee; that thou mayest inherit the land wherein thou art a stranger, which God gave unto Abraham.
Genesis 28:4

Strangers shall bless me. I shall have inheritance in the place that God has positioned me. Wherever my feet go as of today, the rulers, heads and leaders of such places shall be favourable unto me, in the Mighty Name of Jesus, Amen.

Day 6
Favour

And he said, let me go, for the day breaketh. And he said, I will not let thee go, except thou bless me. And he said unto him, What is thy name? And he said, Jacob. And he said, Thy name shall be called no more Jacob, but Israel: for as a prince hast thou power with God and with men, and hast prevailed.

Genesis 32:26-28

I shall never be a reproach in the land, for my name shall find favour with Almighty God and men, in the Mighty Name of Jesus, Amen.

Day 7
Triumph

Thou shalt not be afraid for the terror by night; nor for the arrow that flieth by day; Nor for the pestilence that walketh in darkness; nor for the destruction that wasteth at noonday. A thousand shall fall at thy side, and ten thousand at thy right hand; but it shall not come nigh thee.
Psalm 91:5-7

The strength of the Lord shall be my portion, for I shall prevail over my enemies who shall fall at my side and at my right hand. No terror, arrow, pestilence or destruction shall come near me or my dwelling place, in the Mighty Name of Jesus, Amen.

Day 8
Good Health

And ye shall serve the Lord your God, and he shall bless thy bread, and thy water; and I will take sickness away from the midst of thee.
Exodus 23:25

All the days of my life, I shall be blessed with healthy food. No sickness or disease shall be a part of my body, in the Mighty Name of Jesus, Amen.

Day 9
Understanding

I will bless the Lord, who hath given me counsel:
my reins also instruct me in the night seasons.
Psalm 16:7

I shall be blessed with the wisdom, knowledge and counsel of the Lord in every season of my life, in the Mighty Name of Jesus, Amen.

Day 10
Earthly Treasures

Then shall the earth yield her increase; and God, even our own God, shall bless us.
Psalm 67:6

The earth shall yield its increase of blessings into my life and I shall enjoy the abundance of its treasures, in the Mighty Name of Jesus, Amen.

Day 11
Spirit of Praise

And David said to all the congregation, Now bless the Lord your God. And all the congregation blessed the Lord God of their fathers, and bowed down their heads, and worshipped the Lord, and the king.
1 Chronicles 29:20

My lips shall bless the Lord continually. No guile or evil speaking shall be found in my mouth, for the praise of my God shall flow from within me like a continuous fountain, in the Mighty Name of Jesus, Amen.

Day 12
Protection

The Lord hath been mindful of us: he will bless us; he will bless the house of Israel; he will bless the house of Aaron.
Psalm 115:12

The thoughts of the Lord shall ever be towards me, therefore, no evil projections can prevail against my life, in the Mighty Name of Jesus, Amen.

Day 13
Storehouse Increase

The Lord shall command the blessing upon thee in thy storehouses, and in all that thou settest thine hand unto; and he shall bless thee in the land which the Lord thy God giveth thee.
Deuteronomy 28:8

My financial and spiritual storehouses shall multiply as of today. Anything my hands touch shall become fruitful, extraordinary and exceptional, in the Mighty Name of Jesus, Amen.

Day 14
Glorious Shield

Blessed shalt thou be in the city,
and blessed shalt thou be in the field
Deuteronomy 28:3

The favour of the Lord shall be upon me in this city and in every place; for the glory of the Lord shall surround me like a shield, in the Mighty Name of Jesus, Amen.

Day 15
Unceasing Blessings

Blessed shalt thou be when thou comest in, and blessed shalt thou be when thou goest out.
Deuteronomy 28:6

When I rise up, favour, kindness, love, and compassion shall be towards me. When I lie down, my name shall be spoken of kindly as blessings shall be uttered over me, in the Mighty Name of Jesus, Amen.

Day 16
Divine Direction

Blessed is the man that walketh not in the counsel of the ungodly, nor standeth in the way of sinners, nor sitteth in the seat of the scornful.
Psalm 1:1

My feet shall not walk in the ways of the counsel of wicked men, neither shall the pathway of wickedness be revealed unto me, in the Mighty Name of Jesus, Amen.

Day 17
Preservation

The Lord shall preserve thee from all evil: He shall preserve thy soul. The Lord shall preserve thy going out and thy coming in from this time forth, and even for evermore.
Psalm 121:7-8

The plans of the evil ones shall never catch me because my soul is preserved in the hand of the Lord who protects me from day to day, in the Mighty Name of Jesus, Amen.

Day 18
No Sorrow

The blessing of the Lord, it maketh rich, and he addeth no sorrow with it.
Proverbs 10:22

Riches shall be my portion because the dew of heaven shall soak my life, and no sorrow shall be found in my camp, in the Mighty Name of Jesus, Amen.

Day 19
Divine Reversal

Nevertheless the Lord thy God would not hearken unto Balaam; but the Lord thy God turned the curse into a blessing unto thee, because the Lord thy God loved thee.
Deuteronomy 23:5

The love of the Lord shall surround me daily, and every curse uttered against me shall be turned into a blessing, in the Mighty Name of Jesus, Amen.

Day 20
Satisfaction

And of Naphtali he said, O Naphtali, satisfied with favour, and full with the blessing of the Lord: possess thou the west and the south.
Deuteronomy 33:23

I shall be satisfied with the favour and full blessings of the Lord, in the Mighty Name of Jesus, Amen.

Day 21
Prosperity

And of Asher he said, Let Asher be blessed with children; let him be acceptable to his brethren, and let him dip his foot in oil.
Deuteronomy 33:24

I shall be blessed with children. Rejection shall be far from me and my family, and I will dip my feet in the oil of the earth, in the Mighty Name of Jesus, Amen.

Day 22
Defence & Safety

The eternal God is thy refuge, and underneath are the everlasting arms: and he shall thrust out the enemy from before thee; and shall say, Destroy them. Israel then shall dwell in safety alone: the fountain of Jacob shall be upon a land of corn and wine; also his heavens shall drop down dew.
Deuteronomy 33:27-28

The arm of the Lord shall be my refuge. He shall be my defence from mine enemies so they cannot touch me, in the Mighty Name of Jesus, Amen.

Day 23
Good Health

But unto you that fear my name shall the Sun of righteousness arise with healing in his wings; and ye shall go forth, and grow up as calves of the stall.
Malachi 4:2

Good health and long life shall be my portion, for Jehovah Rapha shall be my defence, in the Mighty Name of Jesus, Amen.

Day 24
Miracles

How God anointed Jesus of Nazareth with the Holy Ghost and with power: who went about doing good, and healing all that were oppressed of the devil; for God was with him.
Acts 10:38

My going forth shall be filled with miracles. The Lord shall work through me, and many shall experience the supernatural of God through my life, in the Mighty Name of Jesus, Amen.

Day 25
Spiritual Blessings

Blessed be the God and Father of our Lord Jesus Christ, who hath blessed us with all spiritual blessings in heavenly places in Christ.
Ephesians 1:3

My days shall be blessed with the spiritual blessings from heaven above, in the Mighty Name of Jesus, Amen.

Day 26
Covering

For thou, Lord, wilt bless the righteous; with favour wilt thou compass him as with a shield.
Psalm 5:12

Righteousness shall be my garment and favour my shield, in the Mighty Name of Jesus, Amen.

Day 27
Good Desires

Thou hast given him his heart's desire, and hast not withholden the request of his lips. For thou preventest him with the blessings of goodness: thou settest a crown of pure gold on his head.
Psalm 21:2-3

A crown of pure gold shall be upon my head. The good desires of my heart shall come to me and the requests of my lips shall be granted by the Lord, in the Mighty Name of Jesus, Amen.

Day 28
Rich Provision

And my God shall supply every need of yours according to his riches in glory in Christ Jesus.
Philippians 4:19

All my needs shall be supplied. The glory of the Lord shall perform this, and great shall be my peace, in the Mighty Name of Jesus, Amen.

Day 29
Eternal Life

And I give unto them eternal life; and they shall never perish, and no one shall snatch them out of my hand.
John 10:28

My name shall be written in the Book of Life. Hell shall not be my destination, in the Mighty Name of Jesus, Amen.

Day 30
Material Increase

Blessed shalt thou be when thou comest in, and
blessed shalt thou be when thou goest out.
Deuteronomy 28:6

My family and I will increase in material possessions. Lack shall not be a part of me. Abundance is our portion, in the Mighty Name of Jesus, Amen.

Day 31
Fruitfulness

And he shall be like a tree planted by the streams of water, That bringeth forth its fruit in its season, Whose leaf also doth not wither; And whatsoever he doeth shall prosper.

Psalm 1:3

Oh God bless me with prosperity in my finances, health, career, business, ministry and family, in the Mighty Name of Jesus, Amen.

Day 32
Gladness

Thou hast put gladness in my heart, more than they have when their grain and their new wine are increased.
Psalm 4:7

Oh God bless me with gladness, in the Mighty Name of Jesus, Amen.

Day 33
Strong Foundation

If the foundations be destroyed, what can the righteous do?
Psalm 11:3

Oh God bless me with a strong foundation, in the Mighty Name of Jesus, Amen.

Day 34
Peace & Safety

In peace will I both lay me down and sleep; for thou, Jehovah, alone makest me dwell in safety.
Psalm 4:8

Oh God bless me with peace and safety, in the Mighty Name of Jesus, Amen.

Day 35
Thanksgiving

That I may make the voice of thanksgiving to be heard, and tell of all thy wondrous works.
Psalm 26:7

Oh God bless me with the voice of thanksgiving, in the Mighty Name of Jesus, Amen.

Day 36
Laughter

All they that see me laugh me to scorn: They shoot out the lip, they shake the head, saying, Commit thyself unto Jehovah; let him deliver him: Let him rescue him, seeing he delighteth in him. But thou art he that took me out of the womb.
Psalm 22:7- 9

Oh God bless me with laughter in the midst of my struggles, in the Mighty Name of Jesus, Amen.

Day 37
Honour

His glory is great in thy salvation: Honour and majesty dost thou lay upon him.
Psalm 21:5

Oh God bless me with honour in the land, in the Mighty Name of Jesus, Amen.

Day 38
Great Reward

Moreover by them is thy servant warned: and in keeping of them there is great reward.
Psalm 19:11

Oh God, by your Word, bless me with great reward, in the Mighty Name of Jesus, Amen.

Day 39
Hidden Treasures

And I will give thee the treasures of darkness, and hidden riches of secret places, that thou mayest know that I, the LORD, which call thee by thy name, am the God of Israel.
Isaiah 45:3

Oh God bless me with hidden treasures, in the Mighty Name of Jesus, Amen.

Day 40
Abundant Life

You make known to me the path of life; in your presence there is fullness of joy; at your right hand are pleasures forevermore.
Psalm 16:11

Oh God bless me with abundant life, in the Mighty Name of Jesus, Amen.

Day 41
Strength

He croucheth, and humbleth himself, that the poor may fall by his strong ones.
Psalm 10:10

Oh God bless me with strength that I may not be a victim to the enemy, in the Mighty Name of Jesus, Amen.

Day 42
Good Success

This book of the law shall not depart out of thy mouth; but thou shalt meditate therein day and night, that thou mayest observe to do according to all that is written therein:
for then thou shalt make thy way prosperous, and then thou shalt have good success.
Joshua 1:8

Oh God bless me with success in my daily endeavours, in the Mighty Name of Jesus, Amen.

Day 43
Bright Future

The Lord is the portion of mine inheritance and of my cup: thou maintainest my lot. The lines are fallen unto me in pleasant places;
yea, I have a goodly heritage.
Psalm 16:5-6

Oh God bless me with inheritance and a bright future, in the Mighty Name of Jesus, Amen.

Day 44
Deliverance

The Lord is my rock, and my fortress, and my deliverer; my God, my strength, in whom I will trust; my buckler, and the horn of my salvation, and my high tower.
Psalm 18:2

Oh God bless me with deliverance from my enemies, in the Mighty Name of Jesus, Amen.

Day 45
Purity

Who shall ascend into the hill of the Lord? Or who shall stand in his holy place? He that hath clean hands, and a pure heart; who hath not lifted up his soul unto vanity, nor sworn deceitfully. He shall receive the blessing from the Lord, and righteousness from the God of his salvation.
Psalm 24:3-5

Oh God bless me with clean hands and pure heart, in the Mighty Name of Jesus, Amen.

Day 46
Creativity

In the beginning God created the heavens
and the earth.
Genesis 1:1

Oh God bless me with creative abilities, in the Mighty Name of Jesus, Amen.

Day 47
Promotion

For promotion cometh neither from the east, nor from the west, nor from the south. But God is the judge: he putteth down one, and setteth up another.
Psalm 75:6-7

Oh God bless me with promotion in all areas of my life, in the Mighty Name of Jesus, Amen.

Day 48
Contentment

But godliness with contentment is great gain.
1 Timothy 6:6

Oh God bless me with the spirit of contentment, in the Mighty Name of Jesus, Amen.

Day 49
Angelic Protection

The angel of the Lord encampeth round about them that fear him, and delivereth them.
Psalm 34:7

Oh God bless me with angelic protection, in the Mighty Name of Jesus, Amen.

Day 50
Voice of Authority

The voice of the Lord is powerful; the voice of the Lord is full of majesty.
Psalm 29:4

Oh God bless me with a voice of power and authority, in the Mighty Name of Jesus, Amen.

Day 51
Voice of Praise

Let the people praise thee, O God; let all the
people praise thee. Then shall the earth yield her
increase; and God, even our own God,
shall bless us.
Psalm 67:5-6

Oh God bless me with the voice of praise and the increase of the earth, in the Mighty Name of Jesus, Amen.

Day 52
Light and Salvation

The Lord is my light and my salvation; whom shall I fear? the Lord is the strength of my life; of whom shall I be afraid?
Psalm 27:1

Oh God bless me with your light, salvation, boldness, and assurance, in the Mighty Name of Jesus, Amen.

Day 53
God's Goodness

Oh that men would praise the Lord for his goodness, and for his wonderful works to the children of men!
Psalm 107:15

Oh God bless me with your goodness and wonderful works, in the Mighty Name of Jesus, Amen.

Day 54
Enduring Mercies

O give thanks unto the Lord; for he is good: because his mercy endureth for ever.
Psalm 118:1

Oh God bless me with your enduring mercies, in the Mighty Name of Jesus, Amen.

Day 55
Stability

Surely he shall not be moved for ever: the righteous shall be in everlasting remembrance.
Psalm 112:6

Oh God bless me with stability in all areas of my life, in the Mighty Name of Jesus, Amen.

Day 56
Breakthrough

I will go before thee, and make the crooked places straight: I will break in pieces the gates of brass, and cut in sunder the bars of iron:
Isaiah 45:2

Oh God bless me with breakthrough in my education, career, business, finances, marriage, family and ministry, in the Mighty Name of Jesus, Amen.

Day 57
Fruit of the Womb

Lo, children are an heritage of the Lord: and the fruit of the womb is his reward. As arrows are in the hand of a mighty man;
so are children of the youth.
Psalm 127:3-4

Oh God grant unto me children who are blessed, anointed, confident, and favoured in the nations so that in my old age I will not be disappointed, in the Mighty Name of Jesus, Amen.

Day 58
Skillful Hands

He teacheth my hands to war, so that a bow of steel is broken by mine arms.
Psalm 18:34

Oh God bless my hands with supernatural skills, in the Mighty Name of Jesus, Amen.

Day 59
Direction

Thy word is a lamp unto my feet,
and a light unto my path.
Psalm 119:105

Oh God bless me with your Word and direction in my life, in the Mighty Name of Jesus, Amen.

Day 60
His Presence

O send out thy light and thy truth: let them lead me; let them bring me unto thy holy hill, and to thy tabernacles.
Psalm 43:3

Oh God bless me with your light in my life and guide me into your Presence, in the Mighty Name of Jesus, Amen.

Day 61
Fulfilled Destiny

Be not over much wicked, neither be thou foolish: why shouldest thou die before thy time?
Ecclesiastes 7:17

My destiny shall never be aborted. I shall not die before my time, in the Mighty Name of Jesus, Amen.

Day 62
Daily Preservation

The Lord shall preserve thy going out and thy coming in from this time forth, and even for evermore.
Psalm 121:8

My going out is prosperous and my coming in is filled with abundance of blessings, in the Mighty Name of Jesus, Amen.

Day 63
Provision and Support

Provide neither gold, nor silver, nor brass in your purses, nor scrip for your journey, neither two coats, neither shoes, nor yet staves: for the workman is worthy of his meat.
Matthew 10:9-10

Wherever my journey takes me in life, abundant provisions shall always be made for me, in the Mighty Name of Jesus, Amen.

Day 64
Answered Prayers

And it shall come to pass, that before they call,
I will answer; and while they are yet speaking,
I will hear.
Isaiah 65:24

Every answer to my prayers shall be granted and will come to me speedily, in the Mighty Name of Jesus, Amen.

Day 65
Unhindered Movement

Every valley shall be filled, and every mountain and hill shall be brought low; and the crooked shall be made straight, and the rough ways shall be made smooth.
Luke 3:5

I shall have unhindered movement because the difficult areas and rough places of my life have now become smooth, in the Mighty Name of Jesus, Amen.

Day 66
Glory-Realm of Prosperity

Beloved, I wish above all things that thou mayest prosper and be in health, even as thy soul prospereth.
3 John 2

I have stepped into the glory-realm of prosperity, in the Mighty Name of Jesus, Amen.

Day 67
Generational Blessings

Praise ye the Lord. Blessed is the man that feareth the Lord, that delighteth greatly in his commandments. His seed shall be mighty upon earth: the generation of the upright shall be blessed. Wealth and riches shall be in his house: and his righteousness endureth for ever.
Psalm 112:1-3

Wealth and riches shall be in my house and my generations, in the Mighty Name of Jesus, Amen.

Day 68
Empowerment

But thou shalt remember the Lord thy God: for it is he that giveth thee power to get wealth, that he may establish his covenant which he sware unto thy fathers, as it is this day.
Deuteronomy 8:18

I am empowered by the Spirit of God to get wealth all the days of my life, in the Mighty Name of Jesus, Amen.

Day 69
Joy

Thou wilt shew me the path of life: in thy presence is fullness of joy; at thy right hand there are pleasures for evermore.
Psalm 16:11

The presence of Jehovah is with me continually to give me joy, in the Mighty Name of Jesus, Amen.

Day 70
Safe Journey

Then shalt thou walk in thy way safely, and thy foot shall not stumble.
Proverbs 3:23

I will walk in safety and shall never stumble or fall in any area of my life, in the Mighty Name of Jesus, Amen.

Day 71
Victory

The Lord said unto my Lord, Sit thou at my right hand, until I make thine enemies thy footstool.
Psalm 110:1

By the power of the Almighty God, the enemies of my life shall become my footstool, in the Mighty Name of Jesus, Amen.

Day 72
Anointing

I have found David my servant; with my holy oil have I anointed him: With whom my hand shall be established: mine arm also shall strengthen him.
Psalm 89:20-21

By the grace of God, I am anointed to carry out the purpose of God in the earth, in the Mighty Name of Jesus, Amen.

Day 73
Deep Roots

As ye have therefore received Christ Jesus the Lord, so walk ye in him: Rooted and built up in him, and stablished in the faith, as ye have been taught, abounding therein with thanksgiving.
Colossians 2:6-7

I and my household shall be rooted and grounded in Christ, in the Mighty Name of Jesus, Amen.

Day 74
Delight

But the meek shall inherit the earth; and shall delight themselves in the abundance of peace.
Psalm 37:11

My mornings shall burst forth with great possessions, good health, abundance and peace, in the Mighty Name of Jesus, Amen.

Day 75
God's Judgement

Thou shalt make them as a fiery oven in the time of thine anger: the Lord shall swallow them up in his wrath, and the fire shall devour them.
Psalm 21:9

The fire shall of the Lord shall consume the enemies who seek to destroy my soul, in the Mighty Name of Jesus, Amen.

Day 76
Cleansing

Who can understand his errors? cleanse thou me
from secret faults.
Psalm 19:12

Every secret fault in my life that the devil could use against me to cause limitation is permanently removed, in the Mighty Name of Jesus, Amen.

Day 77
Overcoming the Accuser

Break their teeth, O God, in their mouth: break out the great teeth of the young lions, O Lord. Let them melt away as waters which run continually: when he bendeth his bow to shoot his arrows, let them be as cut in pieces. As a snail which melteth, let every one of them pass away: like the untimely birth of a woman, that they may not see the sun

Psalm 58:6-8

Every accusation against my life that has caused mountains and obstacles to stand in my way shall melt before me, in the Mighty Name of Jesus, Amen.

Day 78
Youthful Renewal

Who satisfieth thy mouth with good things; so that thy youth is renewed like the eagle's.
Psalm 103:5

The Lord shall satisfy me with good things so that my youthfulness is renewed like an eagle's, in the Mighty Name of Jesus, Amen.

Day 79
Indwelling Peace

The Lord will give strength unto his people; the Lord will bless his people with peace.
Psalm 29:11

The Lord shall cause peace to continually dwell in my house, ministry, workplace, community and nation, in the Mighty Name of Jesus, Amen.

Day 80
Restoration

Men do not despise a thief, if he steal to satisfy his soul when he is hungry; But if he be found, he shall restore sevenfold; he shall give all the substance of his house.
Proverbs 6:30-31

Whatever the enemy has stolen from me is now returned. I shall have seven years increase and restoration in one year, in the Mighty Name of Jesus, Amen.

Day 81
Overflow

And the floors shall be full of wheat, and the vats shall overflow with wine and oil.
Joel 2:24

By the grace of the Lord, I shall experience an overflow of goodness in all areas of my life, in the Mighty Name of Jesus, Amen.

Day 82
Fruitful Labour

For thou shalt eat the labour of thine hands: happy shalt thou be, and it shall be well with thee.
Psalm 128:2

I shall benefit from my labour and it shall be well with me and all that concerns my life and family, in the Mighty Name of Jesus, Amen.

Day 83
Divine Selection

And the angel answered and said unto her, The Holy Ghost shall come upon thee, and the power of the Highest shall overshadow thee: therefore also that holy thing which shall be born of thee shall be called the Son of God.
Luke 1:35

The Spirit of the Lord shall overshadow me with the power of the Most High God that I may be a carrier of the glory of God, in the Mighty Name of Jesus, Amen.

Day 84
Weapons of War

Thou art my battle axe and weapons of war: for with thee will I break in pieces the nations, and with thee will I destroy kingdoms;
Jeremiah 51:20

I am God's battle axe and weapon of war, in the Mighty Name of Jesus, Amen.

Day 85
Cancellation

No weapon that is formed against thee shall prosper; and every tongue that shall rise against thee in judgment thou shalt condemn. This is the heritage of the servants of the Lord, and their righteousness is of me, saith the Lord.
Isaiah 54:17

Every evil weapon fashioned against me for mischief shall perish and not prosper, in the Mighty Name of Jesus,
Amen.

Day 86
Disgracing the Enemy

Blotting out the handwriting of ordinances that was against us, which was contrary to us, and took it out of the way, nailing it to his cross; And having spoiled principalities and powers, he made a shew of them openly, triumphing over them in it.
Colossians 2:14-15

Every demonic handwriting and limitation against my progress is disgraced, in the Mighty Name of Jesus,
Amen.

Day 87
Divine Immunity

They shall take up serpents; and if they drink any deadly thing, it shall not hurt them; they shall lay hands on the sick, and they shall recover.
Mark 16:18

Deadly things shall not harm me,
in the Mighty Name of Jesus,
Amen.

Day 88
Supernatural Flow

Insomuch that they brought forth the sick into the streets, and laid them on beds and couches, that at the least the shadow of Peter passing by might overshadow some of them.

Acts 5:15

Signs, wonders, miracles and the supernatural shall follow me, in the Mighty Name of Jesus, Amen.

Day 89
Prophetic Insight

And he said, Hear now my words: If there be a prophet among you, I the Lord will make myself known unto him in a vision, and will speak unto him in a dream.
Numbers 12:6

I shall clearly hear the voice of the Lord in visions and dreams, in the Mighty Name of Jesus, Amen.

Day 90
Quick Manifestation

Then said the Lord unto me, Thou hast well seen:
for I will hasten my word to perform it.
Jeremiah 1:12

All righteous decrees over my life shall be hastened to manifestation by the Lord, in the Mighty Name of Jesus, Amen.

Prophetic Decrees over Your Life

THE DECLARATIONS OF an anointed servant of the Lord over your life is very powerful. When such decrees are released there is an activation of grace over your life that causes such words to go to work on your behalf in the realms of the spirit. God honours the words of His servants and will reinforce it with His power. I pray that God will do the same for you today as you read these prophetic declarations over your life, coming from my heart to you.

As a prophet of God, I decree that:

- *Your enemies shall be brought low. Those that seek your shame shall be confounded and fall by their own deceit and trickery (Ps. 7:10-17).*

- *The Lord shall fight for you as you remain upright before Him (Ps. 35:1).*

- *The goodness of life is upon you. You shall live and not die to declare the works of the Lord (Ps. 23:6; Ps. 118:17).*

- *This generation shall call you blessed and you shall be honoured in the land (Ps. 112:2; Zeph. 3:19).*

- *Your name shall be established in the earth and you shall be favoured amongst great men (Prov. 3:4).*

- *You shall dip your feet in the oil of plenty. The abundance of the earth shall be yours (Deut. 33:24).*

- *You shall never lack money and resources to accomplish your tasks in life (Ps. 34:9-10).*

- *Every seed that you have planted will bear fruit in abundance (Isa. 30:23).*

- *The Heavens shall be opened over your life (Deut. 28:12).*

- *The Lord shall not be far from you. He will be your present help in all situations and circumstances of life (Ps. 27).*

In the Mighty Name of Jesus, Amen.

About The Author

Bernard W. Deslandes is an Ordained Pastor, Bible Teacher, Conference and Seminar speaker, Spiritual Warfare and Deliverance Minister, and Author who operates on the platform of the prophetic grouping of gifts. He has an unquenchable passion for seeing the oppressed delivered and those who are bound set free. He has authored the books *'10 Times Better: Breaking Spiritual Limitations Against My Educational Progress'* and *'10 Times Better: Personal Reflective Journal'*.

He holds a Bachelors in Divinity from Christian Leaders Institute, Michigan USA; a Masters of Theology from Regency School of Ministry and Missions, Canada & Covenant School of Ministry and Divinity, Philippines.

Prophet Bernard has ministered in Jamaica, several Caribbean Islands, and the United States. He is married and the father of two boys.

Other Books by Bernard W. Deslandes

The prayers and revelations throughout this book are taken from the life of Daniel and the three Hebrew Boys, Hananiah, Mishael and Azariah – young men who exhibited tremendous academic qualities and achieved great results because of their commitment to God. They had a lifestyle of prayer and faith. This faith ultimately catapulted them to become 10 TIMES BETTER.

If you are ready to improve in your learning or to see your children improve, this book is definitely for you. Break barriers, remove obstacles and overcome limitations that have been standing in the way of your intellectual capabilities and progress.

ISBN: 978-976-96025-0-2
EBook ISBN: 978-976-96025-1-9

Available on Amazon

10 Times Better takes you on a journey of discovering the spiritual obstacles and hindrances to one's educational pursuits.

In this *Personal Reflective Journal*, you are able to personally map your own progress and development as you delve deeper into 10 Times Better and actively reflect on key issues relating to your educational pursuits. It will help you to do some soul searching, prayer, and unearthing of those things that you may not have thought about before. When you are done, you will be able to practically see where you are and have keen insights to be able to make adjustments to become 10 Times Better.

ISBN: 978-976-96025-2-6

Available on Amazon

For further Information or to Book Prophet Bernard for your Seminar, Conference, or Church:

www.prophetbernardministries.org

prophetbernardministries@gmail.com

https://www.facebook.com/bernard.deslandes

@prophetbern_min

57391787R00066

Made in the USA
Middletown, DE
30 July 2019